Animals Are Shouting Down From the Sky

Poems

Genevieve Greinetz

Ben Yehuda Press
Teaneck, New Jersey

ANIMALS ARE SHOUTING DOWN FROM THE SKY ©2025 Genevieve Greinetz. All rights reserved. No part of this book may be used or reproduced in any manner whatsoever without written permission except in the case of brief quotations embodied in critical articles and reviews.

Published by Ben Yehuda Press
122 Ayers Court #1B
Teaneck, NJ 07666

http://www.BenYehudaPress.com

To subscribe to our monthly book club and support independent Jewish publishing, visit https://www.patreon.com/BenYehudaPress

Jewish Poetry Project #55   http://jpoetry.us

Ben Yehuda Press books may be purchased at a discount by synagogues, book clubs, and other institutions buying in bulk. For information, please email markets@BenYehudaPress.com

ISBN13 978-1-963475-74-6 pb

25 26 27 28 / 10 9 8 7 6 5 4 3 2 1   250226

For my favorite animal, Yogi
May his memory be for blessing

Acknowledgements

Jokes Literary: version of The Bathroom at Manny's
Voicemail Poems: version of The Bathroom at Manny's
Honey Literary: Anxious Body is a Zoo of Similes
NOMADartX:
    version of Anxious Body is a Zoo of Similes
    Hot Soup
NELLE: A Piece of the Disappearing
Pink Disco:
    version of Imagining Imagination
    To Metabolize a Man
Lady Book Witch Press:
    Breast Riff
    Dictionaries were Physical

Contents

Part 1

I Said— / 4
Nature Is Pretty but Monotonous / 6
Opinionated Sky / 8
Playground Fights / 9
Breast Riff / 11
Hot Soup / 13
Dictionaries Were Physical / 14
Nickname / 16
Animals Are Shouting Down From the Sky / 17
Imagining Imagination / 19
Let's Eat Instead of Thinking / 20
Nothing Is Sound / 22

Part 2

It's Weird But / 24
Supposed to Mention / 25
Too Form Fitting / 27
Through the Lint / 29
New Surfboard / 31
Going Down With the House / 33
It's Cool – Be a Man / 34
All That Ended After WWII / 35
You Will Disqualify / 37
Yesterday We Were All in the Water / 39
Stuff & Things / 41
On My Way to the Showers / 43

Part 3

A Piece of the Disappearing / 46
Everyone Is Wearing Patagonia / 47
Traffic / 49
To Metabolize a Man / 50

When Robots / 51
The Way it Really Looks / 53
Prophets / 54
Make Me a Horror Film / 55
Anxious Body is a Zoo of Similes / 56
Dainty Flats / 57
A Last Redwood Even Xanax / 59
CANCELLED / 60
How to Put the Car in Gear / 61
The Bathroom at Manny's / 62

Thank You / 64
About the Author / 65

Animals Are Shouting Down From the Sky

Part 1

I Said—

You know you could get killed
for saying that– i know people
who would burn your house

up for saying that and i do. We'd been
on the couch, i had to go and left reading
Bukowski knowing i could die

for reading poems like that in San Francisco on the train
where anyone could peer over my shoulder and slit a vein of me
for reading the wrong letter in the wrong way. I'm saying it was tense

on the couch, tense on the train, tense in my office
where i spend the afternoons hearing about hostages
being woven into tunnels they could get killed

for being home. I could get killed
for saying *home* in a line like this at a time like this in a war
that's over there but i could get killed for a war

like this its threats swivel in my mom's mind she calls me
on my way to work afraid i could die in there today like i'm special
agent, undercover secret op status when really i'm standing around

face to the screen, hands on keys emailing grievances and studying
Aramaic and i could get killed
for drinking tea out of a thermos in my office

at the synagogue i could die
standing here, could get killed for verses
like these. Could die for crying at the wrong time over the wrong

person on the wrong couch with the wrong guy–
i could get killed for driving home. My neighbor died
for being a person, I could die

from that, you could get killed for having a thought
like that i know someone who got shot
for saying the wrong thing at the wrong grocery store

to the wrong person trying to buy some ice cream—
you can die for that now, can get killed
for purchasing the wrong flavor.

Nature Is Pretty but Monotonous

Remember 2017 when Trump looked that eclipse
straight in the eyes? It's all the proof I need
to know the planet is a teenage girl

taken by the bad boy since nature is pretty
but monotonous without bad little exhaust fumes
& melting icebergs. And it's too quiet

without wars & airplanes. Planet loves bad. There's a debate
in the Talmud but in the end everyone agrees
that everything would be better were humans not created

at all and yesterday i saw a dead coyote
out the passenger side of my car on Highway 1. I'm so destructive
we all are, but plants are bored without blades of weedwhackers

whirling on shabbes mornings when i'd prefer to complain
than be gracious about what i have. It's that fit of discomfort
that keeps the planet spinning. That whole hate it

but love to hate thing pulling gravity over leaves down to the shoots
& into soils. The planet is in an abusive relationship with me
& my friends. Birds are saying, *Earth you've got to stop this*

love and support for your bad boy human, it's killing you. But the dirt
loves the boot, and the boots don't give a fuck
about anything but steak & even vegetarians

love a barbecue. Earth loves the hate & all this
is bullshit. I used to be a teenage girl. I used to love the bad
men who treated me like I treat the planet and i get it

winter is boring without atmospheric rivers flooding San Diego.
Summer is a drag without the rage of fires
burning up the ridge lines. Being seventeen sucks

Genevieve Greinetz

without motorcycle drunks & the rush of running
for your life, stealing breath
from other creatures. I heard NASA

thinks people will evolve into martians when we colonize Mars.
I heard that red planet's seeking some new flame
since it's bored out there

207 million miles away, pining for a gaze
from some idiot like Trump googly eye looking
at the blind totality light.

Opinionated Sky

What I'm trying to say is Beta Pictoris
got bigger than Polaris. It's like no one

cares about the North Star since NASA
posts all these alluring things like supermassive

black holes & winking galaxies 63 light years
away & i'm trying to say i miss that place

where we used to point and think alright
that's the ethic of the world, and ok

there's the leader, but now it's spiral galaxies
& choose your own principles, moralities— I swear that North

Star used to live in the Pentagon, i'd seen it
swirling on ceilings & in classes

on wisdom texts, but supernovas, the universe
expanding & artificial aliens—it only rains

here seven coves south of Ocean Beach, so far
from city light & still i see nothing up there

on Wednesday night just wind and all America
riffing in an opinionated sky. There's no where

to point to and everyone's pointing. I used to follow
those two blazers in Orion's Belt a little diagonal

& up & there was the guide
light beacon Polaris & all its fables with endings

& beginnings & people i trusted & it's the most
divided world the sky's ever seen. Even stars

won't blink back anymore so many other options.

Genevieve Greinetz

Playground Fights

Used to get high, now we beach walk. Pree laments

it's a workout wandering sand we talk exes & T. S. Eliot

we'd 12th grade read him drinking on the floor & Pree

tried to kiss me, i dodged. We're admitting having pretended

to get Eliot. Pree pretends to be bi

on dating apps to "get girls" *it's working* he reports. We wear gawdy

costumes stitched with apologies for everything. He's Indian

i'm a Jew – victimhood never stretchy enough

to impress the delicate Z's, political corrections

erasing my face, but Pree still recognizes me

says i look the same. We talk politics, careers – at work

my seventh graders cross arm pout

about playground fights, text battles

with ex-best friends. Back in my unelectric day

that was regular but to be correct we practice

trauma-informed mindfulness & they take issue

with breathing since their therapists recommend staying away

from meditation & warn quiet can be dangerous

but concede that phones are safe so we stop breathing

go back to your safe boxes i joke they grab

iPhones it's not funny. Pree is laughing

at how intense i still am says *you're just acting*

like someone who cares, he's kidding. I'm wondering

about that. *You know,* i say to him

i still have the same car i did back then.

Breast Riff

It made a difference this morning when i down
zipped my hoodie on the Zoom call, my teacher
smiled at me more— i only did it habitually. When i think

of my breasts it's not something more than
one time walking through a new moon, summer sky
with my mom stumbling across my shoulders, her
tears drooling down my star lit chest &
when we got to the lake
shattering our whiskey glasses
so we could throw our hands out and scream
into the waters' lost breath about my auntie's breasts
& their cancer. Wonder
what it was like to see through breasts like she
saw life through hers. I think

of high school dressing rooms scheming with my girl
and walking out with silk and lace
under our shirts — our purses full
of menthol cigarettes and her parents' orange
prescription tubes of oxycontin, or what white stuff
we could get for free by keeping our v necks
low, cleavage high. I always needed a bra
to float my plump chest up off my ribs, but the
lacey wire things were pockets for gram
baggies with a lunchtime bathroom line to snort, for cash, for
lighters, for folded notes to hand off in hallways. I think, too,

of this thing i read in one of those crystal shops in Oakland, you
know, down by Lake Merritt with the hip boutiques and beer
gardens that bought people
out of their homes. My then
lover handed me a deck of one of those New
Age sets of cards with the herby images you might
imagine & i drew an old woman whose breasts were eyes,
seeing through her nipples like irises and pupils. Mine were
fastened into a button-down work shirt and held up by some house

boat bra. I don't know what it's like to see through your nips
but i get seen
through my chest professionally. This morning

my teacher was all ears once the zipper went
low. My bra just tight enough to shelve a whole encyclopedia set of
shame, my car keys, and two breasts.

Hot Soup

I heard the BBC news anchor interviewing a scientist
about the age of the universe, some breakthrough

discovery & i was on my way, twisting
through redwoods down Highway 9 to the beach

& the scientist said the universe was a hot soup
until the Big Bang tossed stars into the broth, and the BBC anchor was like,
Why is this relevant?

The scientist coughed. She said, *We're made of that stellar stuff
this is our history, like an ancestry.* I shut the radio off

pulled up to the beach off 41st & got my board
off the roof, walked down into the water and thought

the ocean was howling, but it was women—
3 of them carving down 1 wave. And it was *only* women

out that full moon morning & the tide was rising
& we surfed & shouted & i wiped out

on an overhead wave but it wasn't the lungless tumbling
under the white water that left me breathless

it was the one woman with a torn up wetsuit
telling me how windy it'd been in Los Gatos last night

& how the oaks snap this time of year since they're dried up
and i told her *windstorms freak me out.* She said *Hey*

If it's my time to go, that's how i'll go.
  What else i got to do anyway?

Dictionaries Were Physical

Dictionaries are the most honest havens
circulating our stupid hands. My dad had secretaries

all sorts of them. He owned them Monday
through Friday & one took me to lunch once. She was running

for mayor, she saw me doing coke
in a public bathroom & took pity on me for having a dad

who owned junkyards & all these women & at lunch
we ate things on plates, something more sophisticated

than sandwiches since there were forks & maybe even knives. I knew
this woman was serious, so i asked for extra dressing. She sliced things

looked at me & said *You know your dad is always saying the word 'stupid.'*
What a horrendous word. Don't you say that word

dear girl. I had to sniffle there was stuff running
out of my brain & i coughed & said *yea. That's stupid. Fuck that*

anyway. Her name was Rochelle, she quit
& didn't win the election. I liked her round hips, defined as

curvy and talked at by who they looked good for.
My dad owned her pants. To escape the unstretchy denim

i took mine from department stores since i was skinny & people felt bad
for me & the raggedy bitches i ran around with. We were stupid & lived

our teen years when dictionaries were physical & sometimes they had gold
trim pages & indents for every letter & you could sit one down

on a real coffee table & take your real hands & flip through the a's, the k's,
you could scope the c's and v's & look at all the jargon

Genevieve Greinetz

in its honest mouth with the words blazing around in it's smart length
crisp pages. Those stupid dictionaries

were textured like holy books – Bibles and Qurans
with the thin pages & now i believe

in stupid old books & i'm being honest—
the dictionary says stupid is *showing*

great lack of intelligence or common sense & that to me
is the highest virtue on the brilliant planet

spinning for all us dumbed down humans.

Nickname

Call *void, God* – see it
all over in rain, under it. Over there

bombs. Starvation. It's not that i don't think of Gaza
constantly. Over here, another shooting

in Half Moon Bay. If it weren't raining
i'd have heard it. I've nicknamed *air, ether*—call it *null*

when i'm serious, *God* if there are stars. Bullets
singe in rain wind. It's not that i gave up

on my people. The third graders at synagogue
told me two things at 10 a.m. – first

you have to receive love to listen. Second, i'm special
all of us called special. They asked me to hear

ether. Between drops & thunder
claps i do. We nicknamed *space & time*

mom & pop, God for short. It's not
that i closed off or stopped listening. Air

sings with a tremble. Explosives
taking names. Nickname *nothing, God.*

Animals Are Shouting Down From the Sky

Bad with names, bad with dates like mind collapsed
into god time, jewish god time which is past
present future time you can't say kind of

time. It's today and my office is surrounded by armed guards
regular Friday turned up since bomb threats stand at the bimah
and speak our service back to the rivers, it's shabbat

can i say that? I'm jewish, you ok with me using
that word? It's offensive everything is offensive and the offense
is tripping over the lines and defense is failing and words

float off like clouds, like pillars of clouds that lead us all day
through deserts and places with no gravity the heaviness
only sinks us back to earth at night when we sleep and fly

into Chagall's bible mind here on the earth. Can i say that? Earth
or maybe too political. Chagall, too Jewish, me
a rabbi, you believe me, you offended? We're reading the beginning

of the Torah and the security guards are creating worlds
in their walkie talkies. The static between their comments
sits between lines of Torah a 13-year-old is chanting. In the words

god is creating light and god is seeing that the light is good and the animals
are shouting down from the sky and the fishes are welling
up from the womb of earth can i say that, womb? We

ok? I'm bleeding. When the moon was created i bled, i bleed
with it, you cool with that? People are bleeding
everywhere. We get to the second chapter

one of the guards walks out. Tension kicks its magic
in the air and no one is listening but the teen
is saying that Eve birthed Cain, then Abel

then Cain killed Abel and then Abel's blood
cries to god from the earth. The stream of it
shrieks since blood wasn't created to be spilled

but to flow and then maybe one day quench
the thirst of some other creature deep inside the planet.
Abel is bleeding in the book and god

is mourning, no one else is, just god
sobbing inside wind and into the trees. God is shaking
grief in the pines and sap and fruits are falling

Cain just stands there
after jumping off the edge of the story
and going to a place away from the words

that had been fathomed. He just stands there
after killing somebody, killing his brother
when no one even knew how to cry about something

like that. How could you know how to cry
about something like that
if you'd never cried. God knew. And the security guard is back

and things seem fine and the Torah's getting put away
and our phones
are all off and we don't want to turn them on

since now we know how to cry and we can hear blood
screaming from the earth and god is somewhere
off the page of the story and we don't want to get the news just want to sit

in the blurry place after Abel's death and drink up
a little bit of safety while the static
of the walkie talkie chants its number.

Genevieve Greinetz

Imagining Imagination

I've got a boyfriend in the phone. He lives
up the street in San Francisco. Once
we drank and talked and slept
now we air and fire and text. *It's the new thing*
Rachel tells me. Talking to someone
it's all the rage right now you never see them
just think together in a relatively close knit
sphere of mileage so you could grab the keys
and drive over if needed, but otherwise masturbation.
Otherwise dreams. Otherwise just imagining
imagination. My therapist says this is a pattern
for me. To fuck the unreal. It's just the real
stings. And i've been stung
out in the surf these little jellyfish bump around
one nabbed me with its ass or whatever
stings. I limped out. Put the board
on my head. Stumbled home. You can't get angry
at your therapist or the ocean – they turn it around
and float you in it. So you get stuck
and stung. See the real
stings and my shadow text boy
can't reach me, he doesn't even drive. But i do & tonight
i turn the seat heater on so driving north
is bearable on my jelly stung tush. It's stinging real
out here and the words talk sometimes, too.

Let's Eat Instead of Thinking

No one can make music like Miles Davis because electricity
is the loudest voice in the sky. Used to be birds

but that doesn't matter. I don't want to be scary & i can't write a book
without saying how much everything matters. My legs

can't stand it so i clench my glutes cause i'm scared
i could fall into the trench where i saw five birds & everything that matters

dissolved into dark air. The whole world
is perspiring in California – every monsoon & whirlpool

all the rain is rotting the concrete off its hasty rocker. I can't tell
what Earth is doing but i like when people pray about it. Ayla makes music

about it, choreographs dances about it. I told her i'd seen seven geese
in a V & five dead in the sand earlier. She nodded so i asked her,

> *How does the difference*
> *in the sound of the sky effect your music?*

Ridiculously, she said
as in, let's eat instead of thinking

about sad things. She put the Miles Davis on, she's a bassist so Earth
is her muse, but i am curious about air & how people

say all kinds of curious stuff about me, like i'm too nice, or too boundaried
& not nice enough, or that i murder children in tunnels

under my synagogue. Once i helped my old neighbor
with his groceries, on the way in he asked what i do so i said *i'm a rabbi*

he said, *a Jewess? Your nose is too small to be a Jew – you're too pretty*
but that was years ago, he could be dead by now. Ayla sends me a record

Best of Soukouss Express & says it's uplifting it reminds me of seasons when birds existed.

Nothing Is Sound

The other day this kid at synagogue
asked if a war all the way in the middle east

affects her & we thought about air
strikes, changes we'd noticed in cloud

formations & animals & trees & our skin—
its unstable cells constantly exchanging themselves

with Jupiter & its moons & the matter
in every universe. She let me

know that i had been touched by a storm
on the sea in an ocean on a planet neither she

nor i nor you nor NASA
had fathomed & we agreed

not only was this true but that bombs
don't make sense which is why kids & birds

& trees can't understand what they're doing
or why they would happen at all & i said

*there's no answer to why. Why
is irrelevant — nothing is sound* in the sense

of sense but then we knew everything
is sound & we could hear ourselves & the ocean

not the Pacific but THE OCEAN & she let me know time
is sound, & space, too & that she

& i are little seas & that she likes music
i asked what kind, she said *i think every kind*

has some beauty how 'bout you?
I said *yes – yes that makes sense*

Part 2

It's Weird But

Work call from home & that really loud
grass blower cutter starts flying & singing

its blades all over the lawn & i say *sorry*
to the guy i'm talking to *the sound is inescapable*

& he says *you know someone just started blowing leaves out
my window* & i found that odd. It was odd

today i talked to this woman who advised me to dress myself
in a gold orb for protection she said *do it*

& just believe it. Just believe it? Yes, she said i went to pee
& found it odd that i thought of someone else when i looked

into the mirror afterward & odd that i am home now
on a Friday night when i should be at work but the bomb

threats blew through the elevator
music on our hold line i was asked

to stay home & i find it odd the water
has to be filtered & that the ocean is closed

for 72 hours after rains. It's odd that people are mean
when i order coffee from them or drive in lanes

next to them. Odd my colleagues
are at the synagogue without me. Odd my job

is considered dangerous when all i do is peer around
in old letters & books & talk to you & my friends

about what they dream in me. I find it odd
religion is terrorizing the globe, paying my bills, & feeding

my psyche & it's weird but i'm putting the golden
orb all around me & i'm just believing.

Genevieve Greinetz

Supposed to Mention

No, Matthew, we shouldn't have a word
for peace it should be secondary like we don't really

have a word for air when we're breathing it
just is. I spent hours measuring squash

blossoms against their green counterparts. I spent some time
working through arithmetic with my neighbor's son's kid & I went

to a market where a woman rang me up & she printed me
a copy of her mom's MISSING message to post on some post

i may have known of the subtext saying she was somewhere
under the rubble the bulldozers

in Gaza weren't able to rip through because gas
can't make it into that sliver place i guess i'm not quite supposed

to mention & not quite supposed to mention the word
Israel, nor Palestine, nor Biden, nor America. We shouldn't have a word

for gun for powder for ammo for gas for tanks for blood for rubble.
I had to go get another tea from another café for another hit

of something living something caffeinated since i was trying to blink
and talk at the same time & since i was trying to sit

& stand & act like i did have words for things like *i'm so sorry
for your loss, are your loved ones accounted for, how many times*

in the bomb shelter last night? I left. I went. I sat
at a table next to pumpkin plants the blossoms

oozing their honey bomb insides out into Fall & asking
to live, to become fruits, be things, be beautiful & the afternoon

left & the table was a dark place & the neighbor hollered
over the fence & i went to help because there's nothing else to do

than math with some kid since his dad
can't read & i know how to count 1, 2, all the way

10, 100 even more. We added, subtracted. We divided, we conquered
the homework, I left, I went in not quite ready

to pull a ripe thing, this big
pumpkin on the back deck off its vine i'd rather let its life

spoil unarticulated through its organic sanity & sit
in some peace on the deck, even though it'll go unnamed.

Too Form Fitting

America's in   my mouth – red & blue
lights ready to arrest my tongue

with hints of syllables. No longer able
to say *in love* – it's just nonconsensual, totally lacking

responsibility, so victim-y and they'll get ya like they did me
when i talked about the teacher who assaulted my best friend

in his mid-eighties — it's impressive
the old lion's still got saliva & enough roar

to get around to all the rabbi boys at his mystic feet. I guess
it's all the god stuff swirling in his vitalized hands pumping around

with or without tefillin wrapped all over them. I'll put a box on my head
if it means i can talk to you and God unfiltered, but instead i worry

*can i write a poem like this and still be a rabbi? Can i wear these
ass-hugging pants and present*

appropriate? America's at my door to get a quote
about incidences i may know something about & i answer

in a robe, prefer to nod quiet since speech is worthy of jail time
and i'm losing credit by the ethic – can i say *i'm disappointed,*

i disagree. The country wants me to forgive, be soft, and ethics
are phenomenology. We talk all the time, my friends and i

asking each other how to take care of this & that,
how to merge identities – ourselves

with the pillars we stand for when we're called Rabbi.
Can i write this poem? Can i have these breasts

and some respect? People ask me things like
do you work out? And they call me *honey, baby, kiddo, rabbi.* I can't say

back off since that could be perceived as mean, exclusive,
unwelcoming. Ethical cues drip from the old assaulter

mystic man, compass of something authentic. *Can i have this attitude
and my title?* I've been asked not to say *no*

to elementary kids anymore. The old kabbalist
doesn't know what *no* means

so we don't teach it. We pull our morals
from letters that won't offend anyone and i can't wear these pants

to synagogue anymore – too form fitting, might come across
inappropriate. We don't talk about it.

Through the Lint

Don't give me questions
like *what does liberation mean to you?* It doesn't

mean anything anymore since there's no place
to take ten letters including four of five sometimes six

vowels, dig a several inch hole and plant
them. All the soil is eroded and there's no nutrient

left in language to coax the syllables
toward something living. So don't ask

why this night is different from any other since sirens
pool in the air whether it's Sunday or Monday could be

Tuesday or Wednesday and like any other night cement
cakes up with grit – stuff you take your shoes off

to avoid bringing in the house since the sidewalks
are sick with what the planet has

dizzying in its lungs. Don't sway me to define
what it is i mean if not meaninglessness since eyes

in the room are tearing which is Spring
finding its route no matter the conditions riffing

in the tectonic structure we're stomping and spitting
on. I'll tell you there's buds

opening up in the park. Colors like they make up
names for in crayon boxes. Between the chirps

happening all around folks put their phones down since a photo
can't renew liberation either and there's something

inside our pockets past the plastic

cases and sunglasses and through the lint this mini

cave in there collecting fumbles where two letters
don't quite meet. Down there past the resting phone

in the depth of it this little spot in the pocket
with all the space we need to stop asking.

New Surfboard

I got a new surfboard
& it's sexier than Richard Branson
kite surfing into space with a polaroid

of some comedian actor people feel like they know
because he's on TV, but i feel like i know
Richard Branson because i saw his picture

at sea with a naked woman slithered across his life
jacket, wetsuited back. I feel like i know him
because we both like oceans

but he wrote an article on how to score
a surf session with naked models
& i wrote poems about kelp

forests dying & starfish wasting disease, but Richard Branson
must be healthier than Saturn & the Pacific
since he bought them both & I feel like i know Richard

Branson is happy because his smile
reminds me of the devil Tarot card
in the Rider Waite deck, so he must be content

since he beat the world and Jeff Bezos
to outer space in his own capsule & i feel like i know
he'll outlive the condor population in Big Sur

because i think i read his heart is a plastic island
& that he only eats regurgitated artichokes
i mean, i think that's what he paid for, or what

i heard, but i really feel like i know him
since i took his photo surfing
the Internet & now we're basically orbiting

Facebook together & i'm pretty sure Jeff Bezos

only has his photo taken in black & white
or maybe he's just depressed

because Richard Branson wore nice pants
up to space before he even unzipped his.

Going Down With the House

This morning my ankles woke in seas
up in the loft, on the ceiling – water

chewing cement & houses up. A leak in brain
waves my ocean town drowned

in intellect. We used to have a planet, used to have
bodies now living on opinions & the coastguard

is hiring. 8 a.m. helicopters $20,000 chop
to save a surfer. We pay the tax

like bitter kind neighbors, good citizens
and downstairs the couple

couldn't leave. Feds busted doors down, coaxed them
from Wordle & Pokemon GO. They swam out

annoyed at interruptions and accepting
of warm blankets with clattering thumbs

twiddling on screens. Jim giggled in his high window—
going down with the house. I'm glad

there won't be mice in the gazebo anymore. This was California
now reduced to reels. We are mostly offended

by wood refusing to cooperate for front porch
holiday portraits. These planks were my living

room – still Eddy grinds coffee
in that now underwater mill & the cups

are coming out piping hot.

It's Cool – Be a Man

Be a guy with seven letters in your name, or add some
signatures to the campaign list outside the grocery store

those people asking for a minute, i spend about five precisely
calculating how to avoid them & it never works

so be a dude. One of the ones who opens doors
& then closes them. Or who shuts the toilet lid

over the seat – the tidy closed porcelain
egalitarian type. Be the guy living

that dream to be a tree, one of the ones in a coffee table
book or the National Geographic – get famous

for being an old Joshua or a cut down Sequoia. Champion the man
thing like it's quiet in the city underground or with the noise

cancelling headphones on like we wear on airplanes
over Montana when i say you're my brother, father, sister,

nephew, uncle, grandma, daughter – you be that guy
with a tail at the bar, or the one rolling cigarettes outside

be that boy taking pictures of the bridges every Friday
for a year to see what they rust like. Be a bro

in the water swimming with no wetsuit in the winter
cause it's Wednesday and that's what we do. Knit a quilt

stay at home, cut my bangs, wear shorts & when we fly over Oregon
you say i'm your dad, your cousin, your dog, your friend

the one who didn't check a bag so we jump out
in San Francisco, shut the toilet lids down & close the books.

All That Ended After WWII

Lena introduced me to the spiders
on her patio on my way to get the mail, a package
there for me – yellow shoes to match the yellow stars

on the sweater i'll wear Friday when the other rabbis
and i do our shtick for Purim. Told Lena
about the shoes, the holiday, that we will dress

like Jewish musicians – she laughed. The shtick
hasn't started yet but it's a joke already, saying Jewish
in any sentence makes it funny and saying Jew

means we're talking about something demonic, cheap, or else
describing me, my friends. Note the difference
since she's laughing it doesn't seem like there is one

between cheap, bad, demonic and me, my friends. It's not a problem
for anyone in California. Only an issue if I attempt to publish
anything since Lena and the editors at progressive

journals laugh when Jewish is in a sentence and quit their jobs
if Jew gets inside their zines. It's not a problem
for anyone in the states since it's appropriate

to laugh at a shtick that's not happening, and it's ok to cringe
when I'm introduced as a Jew and laugh like you know me
for being in the tribe. It's a nonissue

since no one is antisemitic anymore. Lena let me know
all that ended after WWII & she asked if she could try the yellow
shoes on. I said no & am relieved

about my misunderstanding — the all-in-good-fun
nonissue that has not been happening
since 1945. After all, Lena only laughed

since i said Jewish & all the editors only quit
because Jew got into their zine and it's not antisemitic
it's just thoughtlessly true – like breath or any other thing

essential to living like blinking & eating & it's not an issue
that Lena said *hah now that's Jewy of you* when i walked off
with the shoebox.

You Will Disqualify

I'll make three points but first apologize
for not being minor enough

to be trusted. I'll say i'm not a nazi
you may tell me to capitalize the word

and let me know that i am and i'll say it's not possible
for Jews to be nazis you'll say that's what a nazi'd say

so i am sorry
for being Jewish and seventy-five percent

straight. You will disqualify
my second point which is a question:

why is it so scary to listen to people
you disagree with? And since i am white

skinned and athletic you will let me know
my privilege is disgusting

my questions horrifying. Since i'm a cis woman
you can't stand how fill-in-the-blank-phobic

my mouth looks when i speak. The fact
a sentence like that could even happen

on a piece of paper and merit to be called poetry
you will cancel since my breasts

are big and natural and now i am performing
feminism sorrowfully

since i talk to men and even people
who have money and think things

i'd never consider. I'll get in the car
steer the fuck out of town

but not like i'm fleeing, like i'm going
somewhere else and i'll make a third point

which is pointless since i can afford my rent
and don't know what concrete smells like

with my faced pressed into it at 3 am just trying
to get some sleep like a real citizen

of this fake place i come home to
and i'll say i'm out

which is my third point, to drive off
to the back of the valley

take a walk through the grass back there
and say sorry sorry sorry to every sound that sings.

Yesterday We Were All in the Water

with goggles i saw 20 bodies all around. We were swimming
it's a quiet revery, it becomes ballet, it's not something

ordinary i guess it was months ago two surfers
went out one came back the humans

grieve. Waters storm — they masticate it's not an argument
who was righteous as in was the ocean right to kill

is the surfer a victim or a colonizer. We don't care
who it was, all 20 of us are on our knees our eyes

stream little seas. We mourn we remember
do you? Those signs on everyone's lawns *love*

is love. all are welcome. science is real. Mine says
DEATH IS DEATH. ALL WHO GRIEVE

ARE WELCOME because i want you to stop calling me any name
& i never want to know yours. It's the sea of you. I'm sick

with selves & starved to grieve. The dust knows every death
is one worth mourning and I don't have a lawn

fuck your sign take my seeds sew me with yours i will never get up
from this beach, the gravity teaches tears

to grow roots & i want to put my hands inside trunks
& trees. I'm saying there's no moral side to be taken just that
      DEATH IS DEATH and my planets

are no higher than grief, nor are they interested
in symmetry or any sides at all. I'm just sad or the air

in me is since somebody drowned & kids
are disappearing & people who say they have names and selves

think about righteousness when their orbit
spins opposite grief. We get in the water again because its morning

all 20 of us and we do the freestyle, the butterfly.
It's not something ethical it's a pulse or something

worth swimming & living for. I'd cry
at the loss of any galaxy. We're only nuclei out here. It's quiet.

Stuff & Things

No stars, but i do have
this container.

Rachel gave it to me
filled up with berries – leftovers

from some dinner
that meant everything even though it was so regular

i don't even know what the occasion was
or who else was there

besides Matthew in an apron
something on the skillet, Natalie debuting

her new new, Eliana telling me
her smart angles, and Rachel

in and out, but always
all in. It's a screw-top

Tupperware, that same brand
pretty much every plastic container is

filled up now with a bar of soap, plus bars
of shampoo and conditioner

for the gym. I use it
three, four, five

times a week. Stuff & things
sit on me like a saddle

telling a horse it's supposed to be useful
but really it's supposed to be an animal, and that's the thing—

this container, i mean, i take it
to the shower, but it's an anti-object, some kind

of a capsule holding an evening i'm pretty sure
happened, but positive now

since i have the plastic
screw-top proof it was all real.

On My Way to the Showers

The naked woman's breasts in the locker room
at the Jewish community gym reminded me to take my clothes off
i'd forgotten to on my way to the showers.

I'd been working out, i'd been on an elliptical and a woman
had come to run next to me – she told me her Czech
husband's family only escaped because a nazi

loved her husband's father, gave him baptismal papers. Everyone else
died. Went to the chambers, the showers i'm on my way there
now at the Jewish community center and my friend called me

on my way, in the car, she's blonde, she's white, she's becoming
a therapist and she asked *how are you in the midst*
of all this Israel everything and to be honest i don't know i've been
    swimming

in the lakes of somebody, bathing off his cliffs and wandering in the
    thoughts
of him and maybe it's because i'd prefer his scent than the blood and wreak
of death all over the planet or maybe i don't want to stop thinking

in the chest of him and have to listen
to the pulse of the planet. Could be i love him could be i can't be face
to face eye to eye with guts and sweats and people's pain melting

into the rising tides. Could be i'd rather drink
his water than lick salt off the earth could be irresponsible could be
crucial. I stripped. I put my things in a duffel bag and walked

to the showers hoping to live, hoping to come out and laugh
it was only water.

Part 3

A Piece of the Disappearing

Yesterday, a big beard, blue helmeted man
swept in front of me and took the wave i paddled for,
he scanned the whole ocean and me but looked through me

as if i were a piece of the disappearing
kelp forest out in the surf. He said *what up*
to all the bros, but i am salt out there

dissolved and some of the men speak to me
like the red board man i talked to this morning.
He likes to surf Manresa and when i said i don't go there

because there's white sharks
he said *Yea, i just don't think about that*
but i think about predators all the time

and sometimes i pace in my house at 3 am
hypervigilant for creatures that might invade my body
But the red board man said *sharks*

blend in pretty well and that we just don't see 'em
which is why i don't go to Manresa or take walks outside my house
at night even though i want to but in the daytime

out in the water it seems like i blend in pretty well too
since the bros take my waves and don't worry
about what they're not seeing.

Everyone Is Wearing Patagonia

The internet tells me everything
i need to know. I go on there and find out

did i get the lease, the contract, the date? I log in
and understand helicopter crashes

happen to basketball players and politicians. You know the Bay
got overtaken by tech. I saw it in increments coming home

for visits from out of state remember once
walking in the Haight with Hannah & seeing 10 guys

riding bikes with Patagonia vests on *they all look the same*
i said to her and we kept walking to her house on Oak

across from the park – you know there's bison in there? Those days
were phone for basic things like calling

to say *hi*, set a plan, say *i had a good time
on the date last night* but now everyone is wearing Patagonia

and hip to the same things since the internet tells us all
what to wear and who to act like. Nothing to think

about anymore. Go online
order dinner, buy a vest, get it delivered

overnight and wear it tomorrow
like everyone else riding bikes

without pedaling since they're electric like my brain
and the car this place used to look different

we all looked different
from each other and clothes

came from stores that we went to but those are all closed down
in San Francisco, you know that place

got overtaken by crime so the shops all closed and my mouth
got overtaken by political corrections so i get vests

online, try and blend in like i'm a techie
even though i still pedal my Jamis up and down the old hills.

Traffic

So, you say the traffic
is too much, can't make it

across the google bridge with "+11 min"
of red streaks on the golden gate map
to come have tea

and hike with me, obviously better plans have crept
into your inbox, but blame the jam. Over here

my neighbor is dangling off the top balcony gyrating
cause he thinks he's fucking some mate whose not there
dangling with him on fentanyl. This is San Francisco

and you didn't drive over because the traffic but you said *if i stay
then i can catch the 4:00 showing of Barbie,*

the traffic – but you know bumper
to bumper — we strangers spend intimate time together.
We're in a religious drought and highway One

is all California's got to sit down next to each other & share
a community ritual spilling of oil, spinning of lithium

in the traffic gathering more popular than any synagogue
on a Shabbat morning. But you wouldn't drive. Not with the risk
of sitting next to so many other people in the same

tied up capital grid loss of control on a Saturday when California
is unhinged & fleeing their homes to belong

anywhere, maybe when we get there,
but the traffic –
we belong to the jam.

To Metabolize a Man

The narrative is pitiful the one
going on and on about the pleasure

of being inside a woman you need to know
what it's like to be a sky

for the stars of someone, depths
for their waters and it's not about love

its alchemy & they don't teach these skills, they don't teach
bodies like this – i'm a school, whole wing

of classrooms churning with what the universe
shakes with at nighttime. Yes

i know what you mean
about everything that gets inside us & let me

be clear – alchemy licks one substance, spits
something different & this is how medicine lives

do you know what i mean–
medicine? I mean being

ground for roots to reach in
and sprouting trees on the inside not baby

making, its shadow weaving pulling all the dark
out of night and slipping it

into beams, gold bumping around
in the veins type of thing. You need to know what it is

to spin sage into oil, cedar into blood. What it's like
to metabolize a man, to *be* the inside.

When Robots

Tracing the north cliff line – curtains
of rain have taken you in, enveloped

San Francisco in its habitat that
fog – tattered now by hotter water & dying

everything. You're hidden in it not even a glow
of the fall of you, San Francisco no scent

of piss or drool or shit on the sidewalks everyone
has a blanket now & it's cold & its damp & its dreary

but the world is & the ocean is & about 2000
years ago someone took a little boat

over Salt Sea & wrote they saw eyes in depths in leagues
of sea a quick flash of contact – same sage said

teach your kid to swim & it'll save them
from thievery

& i'm wondering now
when robots

with their clanking ethereal land origin stories will swim
& thieve & play in waves muted of sound in a sepia haze

of lifeless sea. Fog writes in cursive in the sand, says
it's seen time it's not looking good

but also that it never was. Anyway
i took a boat to the deepest belly

around here about 28
or so miles out & i get it, i saw it

we thought, *whale!* but when nothing surfaced nobody
spoke. It was the depth

& it had eyes & tongues & every letter
of every language & it rippled

& we took nothing.

The Way it Really Looks

Carolyn cut my bangs & i feel self-conscious
about which way to pronounce her name

so i don't say it. She got me ready
for the rest of Wednesday – a lunch

with mom, dinner with a lover. I'd dreamt
my mom was 10 years older than she is and knew

she only had 10 more left & it landed like tall grass anonymous
in a wind brown hillside swaying in California. I had the intention

of savoring – everything. The way it really looks is i pull up
a little late and can't look into the browning leaves

curling on my mom's once green skin so i'm unkind, closed
off & brief in responses. She's been listening to sad music and tells me

she's been anxious. So i write about it later with ropes
knotted up in my larynx & i go to dinner with the big guy

i've been seeing. I'm an actress, he's in my theater— i write about it
later. My mom sends me the musician

she's into – strings more real than short bangs i'd asked
if she'd noticed my haircut she said, *we don't see each other so often.*

Prophets

I went with Winnie to the woods for a tree
she knew the leaves would be budding in February

we went & by the scent of the bark, buds in their downy
pods she could see for twenty years, closing her eyes

she saw forty & said even when San Francisco gets covered
with Daly City & flowers & brackish water pools

the men will lay dormant in trapped imaginings and they will teach
each other about God and they will pray and have their systems

of geometry that came from their mystic prophets. While me and her
and the others will walk paths if not to see grass

then to smell mountains & gain the skill to articulate how air
tastes in different regions of the state that has already begun to swim

in its own oceans. In the leaves
she could see that she would die, which she did, and she remembered

being born and she told me everything
was fixed and completely indeterminate. We drank tea

the leaves looked like beaks of old birds
from the myths we slept in.

Make Me a Horror Film

Outside the hallways reek some corpse
rot in the air & water, ghosts of species

torn out of existence. My kitchen blood
stained, rivulets of the death of my last relationship

smearing its haunt on my cabinets. Lena turns the tv
on screen mirroring some Italian

horror flick — out the window dead things
make night interesting. My mind and Lena's flicker in an hour

maybe two of terror, subtitles of it but there's a smell
manic in the air. Ghosts are in the microwave

where that family of five had one of those butter bags of pop
secret when they got murdered over in the war. I'm thinking tv is scary

Suspiria is. We're watching in black & white i'm not over
the dead birds i saw at the beach today and my cousin

getting ghosted by this man she was living with. Imagination
bleeds its own scent, loses its mythology in air raids & media

coverage. Make me a horror film – put it, project it
on puddles haunting our couch – fresh bloods

pouring in from all around—love and people, birds and sharks,
my plants, the grass dying, all dying. The movies

tell me what horror is – weave the real ghosts
into figments put them back

in imagination they're all spilled out in the ink
of a mourning planet. *I can't watch this* Lena

says so she inhales some weed. I light
a cigarette in fog sky like mirrors.

Animals Are Shouting Down From the Sky

Anxious Body is a Zoo of Similes

Anxiety doesn't know what to do
with my face or where to put
my eyes. We're all at the table
with its wood & its weight & i'm

in my own private flood. Bladder is an octopus
hiding in black rocks & all the primordial waters

well up under my chair, carry me
to de-creation— i'm out to sea while everyone else
is eating dinner. My hips have turned
to wolves gnawing on their hind legs, & it's a zoo

in my shoulders. My hovering hands
are ducks in the marshes by the bay. Please pass

the potatoes, throw me
a life raft, the butter. I'm swept out all the way
across from, next to friends— in my own
rip tide. Veins are channels

starved for water at the low tide. Brain is a box
for worms & they're wriggling & i can't paddle
in from the seas, my feet –

my feet. The ground. My feet.

Dainty Flats

I can't eat
which is why i grocery shop—i see

the green grapes, choose the ones
i want, they're mine, i have

it all – i shop. Get the blue jars
clear ones, too, some vegan, gluten

free scone for $20. People care about me
when I pull my wallet out. I'm important

in the aisles and at the shoe store
where i shove my attitude

into dainty flats i hate – it's what they want
me to wear. So i can look like a rabbi

since i don't with my gold earrings
and usually sneakers. But if i was Yaakov

gold earrings & sneakers is hip. I'm not—
i shop. Head down. Just want

to practice blowing smoke rings because fire
doesn't fit into a shoe size. I'm flames

but they don't think it looks good on me – burning up like that
publicly. A private meeting later

i was asked to change
my clothes. My personality. The way

i like to write poems
about sex and cigarettes. It's not very

rabbinic. I've seen the ones who are
those men with the khakis and white shirts

no ties, but they'll wear the Blundstones i'm not allowed
to wear and they'll look like rabbis. Ones i know

sometimes bring congregants into back rooms
and make the right blessing

before, you know, doing stuff i get into trouble
for writing poems about.

A Last Redwood Even Xanax

Since it's not that cold, everyone is medicated
here in the distant west the neighbor cuts down

a last redwood even Xanax
flushes into the Pacific. I'm on the internet

talking to photos of some guy named Ariel, swiftly losing
interest and my brow is furrowed because i wanted to study

Talmud. The old beast
is bleeding out in my untreated attention span, electrically fatal

to ancient things like Aramaic or how to make a fire
there's medication for things like this, i'm on all of it

since swimming in salt water is soaking in sneezes
toilets, and farm run off, but it's mental health awareness month

so i'm not an ally if i ask questions like *why does everyone i know
have ADHD?* The old book wonders how to walk through a field

without touching dead things. Nearly impossible
without crouching down and blowing through a straw

for the distance. I can't read
for five minutes without picking up my phone

i need a straw, another dip in the ocean. Since it's this month
i won't say to Marie that i think her mind is intact

especially since she's feeling anxious. How did things
get packed into orange bottles like this? I can't ask.

Talmud is busy telling me how to make a wine sack
out of a beaver's stomach lining. Out the window

the redwood's gone. It's started to rain, maybe Adderall
in the drops, ocean is calmed down.

CANCELLED

Got cancelled in meditation class
Aditya hired me to teach, said

i was just like Netanyahu, could she know
i woke up forgetful, was that important? It's hard

to remember. Fling the sheets, get them flat again
after dreams & toss-turning my identity

in different faces — but i'm up now
tucking the blanket into the flat sheet and fluffing up

comforters, pillows – the bolstering it takes to lose diurnal certainties
& be swept apart in unlit drifts. Before class she asked

if i agreed with the borders of her politic, policing me she wanted to see
whether to let me into her mainland or keep me

behind her left side wall. I told the woman nothing
was clear to me, i'd made the bed but my mind was grains

heaped in underwater piles – shallow & deep. *You're unreal* she wanted
me to take a side, take hers, I looked at my hands

twisting them back and forth on camera
so she and Zoom could see the verisimilitude of flesh

metabolized into pixels & algorithms. Rolling her doppelganger
screen eyes, sighing in my speakers *fascist,* she said

i'm letting the students in. We're not talking about Israel. I wasn't talking
about Israel, I was asking everyone

to please say their name and Aditya said to say
something else, i can't remember. I was defining

mindfulness, then meditation, then wondering
if the young folks knew cursive or who they were.

How to Put the Car in Gear

I drive my Golf as often as men
give me advice. My mom said she was impressed

when Rabbi David admitted to not knowing something. I tried it
once when i was teaching the men

asked about history so i said, *i'm not a history person
i don't know* and one of them stood on his chair

whipped the phone right out of his pants & spun
his smart fingers on the correct keys to type the address

for Wikipedia. Everyone shook their heads at me
so i renounced my authority to the man & the mighty

Internet. He explained my class
to me & my students beamed at him

like my mom had beamed at Rabbi David
who became vulnerable when he didn't know. I fessed up

& got demoted. Got in my car
after class & rolled the window down

so one of my students could comment on its color
notice that it was a manual & explain how to put the car

in gear — from past experience. I nodded & rolled
up the window so i could listen to advice on the radio—

how to dress, how to walk, how to wipe
my ass and this is how often i drive my car—maybe 250 miles

a week. San Francisco – Pacifica – San Mateo
I hit the clutch, set the gear, touch the gas

& drive the car just how my student explained it to me
even though i've known how to do this for years.

The Bathroom at Manny's

Yes it's possible to fall in love in three sentences
in line for the bathroom at Manny's, full bladder

rearing to go you do selfless things like let the star of the show
cut you in line, it was Alex Edelman. He was crazed & jogging

on stage but in line he was a white deer, i know
because in 1949 Charles Howard bought 53 albino deer

ten bucks a pop & released them to kill for fun
near Point Reyes, but some survived & i pulled up

a few years ago to a lot in Olema – saw the moon thing glowing
elk reindeer just standing there in my headlights like Alex Edelman

blinking at me sweet in line & i said *you should definitely cut me*, so he said
    couldn't possibly
& i said *go on* & he went since it was 5:30 & the thing was starting

at 5:30 but probably 5:29 i built a house in his dewy gaze & by 5:30
we'd lived our whole lives together in it – real true

love, always for me. I'd say it's my problem but this French philosopher
Gabriel Marcel, said swap "mystery" for "problem," see

what happens. It's my mystery. It is. I never saw his pic & he died
in '73 but i married Marcel when i read that. Love him

like those white deer & Alex Edelman. He came out of the bathroom
white shoes walking at me ten paces like he was styling down the aisle

rings & all with the headlights on & i froze
all wide-eyed deer gaze trying to pry

my boyfriend's hand out of mine.

Genevieve Greinetz

Thank You

Most of these poems were written in a gazebo near the ocean here in California, so a foremost thank you to the Pacific, the surrounding trees and land, the many birds and animals, and the occasional whales.

There are many humans to thank, and, this book would not exist without Matthew Lippman. Matthew, thank you for knowing I could do this from the beginning, for reading and editing hundreds of poems over the years, for being my teacher, mentor, friend, boss (yep), editor, and inspiration for thousands of days, and for your partnership in writing. You are an incredibly skilled writer and teacher, thank you for generously sharing your gifts with me.

Thanks to Anne Germanacos for the many prompts, the belief in my poems, and for holding such an amazing writing group—thank you Wednesday writers! And thanks, Merle Feld, for the conversations, contemplations, and your enthusiasm about this collection.

Big love and thanks to my friends and family. You know who you are. I'm ok with words, but it's hard to adequately articulate how lucky I am to have you in my life. Thank you.

Major thanks, too, to Julia Knobloch for being a five-star editor and human, and to the Ben Yehuda Press.

About the Author

Genevieve Greinetz is a San Francisco based rabbi and poet. Her pieces have been published in NELLE, Honey Literary, and NomadartX, among other journals. *Animals Are Shouting Down From the Sky* is her first full length collection.

www.ingramcontent.com/pod-product-compliance
Lightning Source LLC
LaVergne TN
LVHW041346080426
835512LV00006B/638